THE GOLDEN RULE

Written by Caryn Sonberg

Illustrated by Michelle Dorenkamp

To my parents, for all those midnight snacks and for teaching me how to take care of myself. I appreciate all their hard work and commitment to keeping me healthy.
Caryn Sonberg

For Sweet Pea, with love—Mimi.
Michelle Dorenkamp

2005 Printing • Cat. #2-373 • ISBN 1-55501-777-0

Editor
Dr. Roberta Stathis

Art Direction and Design
Danielle Arreola

Editorial Staff
Patrice Gotsch, Kristin Belsher, Linda Mammano, Rebecca Ratnam, Nina Chun

ive more days 'til my birthday, five more days 'til my birthday," Olive sang slightly off-key as she danced around the kitchen table.

"We know there are only five more days until your birthday, Olive," her mother sighed. "Now please calm down or you are going to bump into something and hurt yourself!"

Olive had been planning a sleepover birthday party for weeks. There would be balloons, cake, pizza, games, and even a piñata. Earlier that afternoon, Olive and her mother went to the party store to pick out the piñata of her dreams. It was a big red ladybug with black spots. "Oh, mom," Olive gushed, "it will be just perfect for the party."

4

All week at school, the only thing Olive could think about was her party. When her teacher, Miss Millie, called on her in class, Olive's only reply was, "Huh?" Her friend Betsy would have to tap her on the shoulder and repeat what Miss Millie had asked.

It was recess time on Friday, and Betsy and Olive were on the swings talking about—what else—Olive's big birthday celebration. "How many girls are coming to your party tonight?" Betsy asked.

"Well, there will be seven people, plus me, so that makes eight. And don't worry," Olive said, "my brother Oliver won't be there to bother us. He'll be at my grandmother's house."

"So who will be there?" Betsy asked.

Olive put out her hand to count. "Julie, Sami, Kayla," she paused, "Claire, Ali, Emma, and you ... and me, of course!"

At the end of the school day, Olive headed straight for the bus. She was so excited she forgot to say hello to the bus driver. As usual, she scurried past her little brother Oliver without even glancing at him. Olive smiled as she stared out the window and imagined what her house must look like filled with balloons, cake, presents, and that beautiful piñata.

When she got home, Olive couldn't believe her eyes. The house looked perfect. Purple balloons covered the hallway. There was a huge cake on the kitchen table. It was covered with purple flowers, and the writing on it said "Happy 8th Birthday Olive." The red ladybug piñata hung from a tree in the backyard, and everything was ready for the party. All she needed now were her guests and their presents.

Ding dong.

It was Betsy carrying her overnight bag and a big purple present with a bright red bow. Olive grabbed the gift and invited Betsy inside.

"All the presents go in my room," Olive commanded.

Ding dong. Ding dong. Ding dong.

Before Olive knew it, all of her friends had arrived and her room was filled with sleepover stuff, giggling girls, and lots of presents. Olive opened her presents first. The beautiful pink ice skates and butterfly-shaped kite were her favorite gifts.

"Girls, I think we'd better go outside and break that piñata," Olive's dad announced. The girls ran outside, and one after another they took a turn trying to hit the piñata. With one grand **WHACK**, Sami broke it wide open and candy flew everywhere.

"Get what you can!" Olive's dad shouted.

The girls scurried and dove for the candy. Kayla piled chocolates into her mouth. Ali quickly opened her bubble gum lollipop. Claire picked up a few treats, put them in her pocket, and quietly made her way into the house.

11

"Where are you going?" Ali called out.

"Oh, I'll be right back," Claire said.
"You guys can have the rest."

Claire picked up her overnight bag and took out a small black case. Olive's mom showed her to the bathroom.

All of a sudden, Sami swung open the bathroom door and said, "I won, I ..." She stopped.

Olive pushed her way through to see what was going on. "What are you guys ..." Olive stopped, too.

The girls looked at each other, quickly shut the door, and ran into Olive's bedroom.

From the hallway, Claire heard Olive say, "She is so weird. I can't believe I invited her to my party." Tears filled Claire's eyes. She wanted to call her dad and have him pick her up. She wanted to go home. Just then, Claire felt a hand on her shoulder.

"What's the matter, Sweetheart?" Olive's mom asked.

Claire didn't want to talk, but she knew she'd better or things might get worse. "I was testing my blood sugar and Olive and the other girls saw me. They think I'm weird."

Olive's mom hugged Claire and said gently, "They just don't understand. Let's explain what you were doing. Don't worry. Everything will be okay." Claire just wanted to disappear, but Olive's mom insisted that they talk to the other girls.

17

Olive was standing in the hallway when she saw her mom walking toward her. Olive burst into her room and jumped on her bed. "Mom, Claire needs to go home. She's acting weird," Olive said. Then she saw Claire standing behind her mother. Olive's mom gave Olive a "you're in trouble" look. Olive wasn't sure what to do.

"Olive, this is not the way we behave toward others. It is very hurtful to talk about people behind their backs— whether they hear you or not." Olive didn't know if her mother was angry, disappointed, or maybe both.

"Claire is going to explain to you what she was doing," Olive's mom said. "Don't be so quick to judge people."

19

Claire took a deep breath and wiped the tears off her face. "Well, I have diabetes," Claire whispered. "And when you walked into the bathroom, I was testing my blood sugar to see if I could eat some candy."

"You see," Olive's mother explained, "Claire has to be careful about what she eats. If she eats too much sugar, her body gets upset and then she doesn't feel good. Claire was being very responsible by taking care of herself."

21

"Gosh," Sami blurted out, "I could never test my blood sugar every time I wanted some candy."

"Do you have to stick a needle in your finger to get blood?" Kayla asked.

"That's kinda weird. I would never do that," Olive announced proudly.

Claire wanted to crawl in a corner and hide. However, she knew she had to face the other girls. She wanted to let them know she was still the nice, fun friend they knew. She wanted them to know that she wasn't weird.

"Actually," Claire said, "if you had to do it, like I do, you would learn how to. It's really not that bad."

All the girls stared at Claire.

"So, can you eat candy?" Ali asked.

"Well, maybe just one piece," Claire said.
"I'll save the rest to share with my sisters."

At first, there was an awkward silence in the room. Soon, however, the other girls were asking Claire a million questions.

Olive's mother could hear the girls starting to
giggle and laugh. Everyone was back in the party
mood—everyone, that is, except Olive.

Olive felt bad for making fun of Claire and for talking about her behind her back. The cake and games and all the presents didn't seem as important anymore.

"Mother," Olive whispered, "I know I hurt Claire's feelings. I don't know why I was mean to her. I feel awful and horrible and terrible."

Olive's mom just listened.

"Mom, Claire must hate me. I would hate me. This is the worst birthday ever."

27

After Olive had said everything she had to say, her mom said, "Olive, have you ever heard of the Golden Rule? Repeat after me ... Do unto others as you would want them to do unto you."

Olive repeated her mom's words. She didn't really understand what they meant, but she figured she'd better listen in case it would help her feel better.

"Olive," her mom explained, "every person in the world is a little bit different. People have different ideas and beliefs and needs." Olive was thinking this was sounding like a boring lecture, but she figured now was not the time to point this out to her mother.

"Claire is a diabetic. She didn't ask to be a diabetic. It just happened to her. She is doing the right things in order to stay healthy," her mother said in a matter-of-fact way. "You should treat people the way you want them to treat you. That's the Golden Rule!"

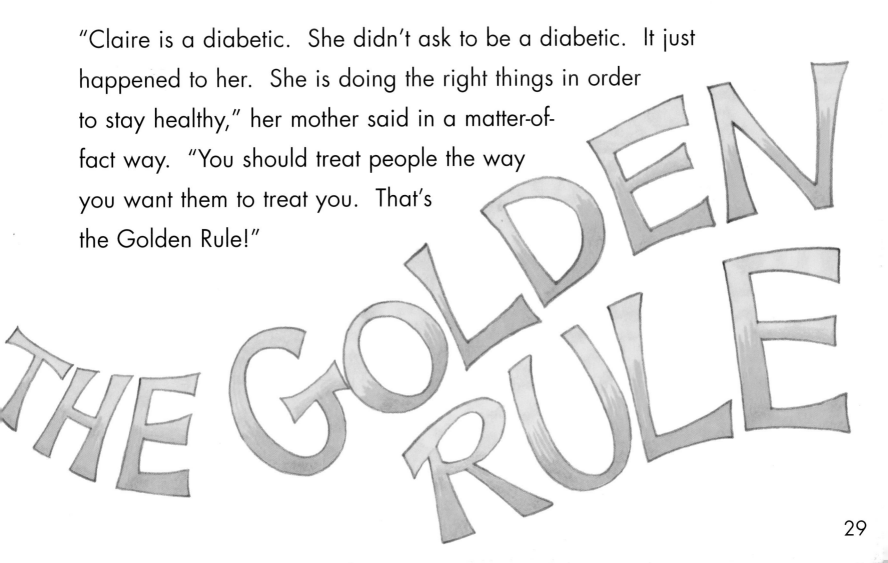

Olive walked back into her bedroom. Some of her friends were watching cartoons. Kayla and Sami had already fallen asleep. Olive climbed into bed next to Claire. "I'm sorry for saying you were weird. I want you to be my friend. I'll never make fun of you again," Olive promised.

Claire smiled. Then she said quietly, "Thanks for inviting me to your party."

Without another word, both Olive and Claire were soon fast asleep.

The End

About the Author

Caryn Sonberg was born in Miami, Florida in 1977. She currently resides in Alexandria, Virginia, where she is a third-grade teacher. When she was a child, Ms. Sonberg spent many summers with her grandmother, Millie. One of her favorite memories of their time together is sitting on the couch listening to her grandmother's "Olive" stories. Each fictional story about a little girl named Olive was tied to a moral lesson. Ms. Sonberg wanted to record the Olive stories to keep her grandmother's tradition alive and share these important life lessons with children everywhere.

This is a photograph of Caryn Sonberg and her grandmother, Millie Sonberg.